These Are a Few of My Favorite Things

Tony D. Burton

To benefit the

Make-A-Wish Foundation®

FIRESIDE
Rockefeller Center
1230 Avenue of the Americas
New York, NY 10020

Designed by Gabriel Levine

Manufactured in the United States of America

1   3   5   7   9   10   8   6   4   2

Library of Congress Cataloging-in-Publication Data is available.

ISBN 0-684-85794-4

The Make-A-Wish Foundation®, based in Phoenix, Arizona, is dedicated to granting wishes to children under the age of eighteen with life-threatening illnesses. It is the largest wish-granting organization in the world, with 81 chapters in the United States and its territories, and 18 international affiliates on five continents. Tony Burton shall donate 3¼% of the book's cover price to the Make-A-Wish Foundation for every copy of the book sold through traditional trade channels, after his expenses have been recouped.

Dedicated to the staff, volunteers,
parents and children of
the Make-A-Wish Foundation®

To my friends, my family,
and, most of all, my Jackie

Acknowledgments

■

First, I would like to thank the Rodgers and Hammerstein Foundation for approving this book's title. It came from my wife's love of the song "My Favorite Things." With the foundation's cooperation, we were able to use the memorable lyric from *The Sound of Music.*

The contributors whose pieces appear in this book also deserve my heartfelt gratitude. Without their participation, this project would never have happened. Having said that, I would also like to thank all the publicists, managers, agents, personal assistants, and friends of the contributors who took my phone calls, faxes, and letters, day in and day out.

Some people I would like to acknowledge by name for going the extra mile to make this happen are: Andrea Miller, Greg Ikonen, Bill Harden, Sarah Longden, Matt Lombardi, Fred Rothenberg, Matt Lauer, Bob Costas, Dave Holbrooke, Greg Picker, David Manns, Andy Zulla, Bonnie Bernstein, Neal Shapiro, and Rebecca Spencer.

Saving the best for last, I would like to thank my editor, Cherise Grant, for her patience, her support, her help, and her lunches. The others at Simon & Schuster who deserve recognition are: Trish Todd, Sue Fleming, Emily Remes, and, last but not least, Helen Adams. Thanks for taking my call.

 Make-A-Wish Foundation®

Dear Friend of the Make-A-Wish Foundation®,

Chris Greicius had a favorite thing—a dream of someday becoming a police officer. A mature seven-year-old with leukemia, Chris had his wish granted when the Arizona Department of Public Safety named him the first and only honorary highway patrolman in state history. This one child's wish was the inspiration behind the founding of an organization dedicated to helping children with life-threatening illnesses realize their one favorite thing. Through Chris's dream becoming a reality, the Make-A-Wish Foundation was born.

Many times in life, we are touched by the actions of a special person, a thoughtful gift, or a heart-warming story. And afterward, our lives are never the same. The indelible mark left by such an experience is something that we treasure and hold dear to our heart for the rest of our lives. It becomes a part of who we are—and who we always wanted to be.

Sometimes, our favorite things come in the shape of something big, like a trip to meet Mickey Mouse or a new computer. Other times, our favorite things may be in the form of less tangible elements—a cool breeze on a warm day, the mouth-watering aroma of a home-cooked meal, or the smile of a child.

Whether your favorite things are big or small, it is important to reflect upon the experiences we so often take for granted. Most of us do not think about the everyday things that make life so special and precious. This book highlights and celebrates some of those things. We hope that in reading it, you will be inspired to ponder fondly a few of your favorite things.

Tony Burton will donate a portion of his profits earned from this book directly to the Make-A-Wish Foundation. Since 1980, we have helped grant more than 65,000 wishes to children with life-threatening illnesses. By purchasing this book, you can join the Make-A-Wish Foundation in granting the wishes of even more children—and help each of our wish kids realize one of his or her favorite things.

On behalf of the Make-A-Wish Foundation and our wish kids, thank you for your support. For more information about the Make-A-Wish Foundation, please call 1-800-722-WISH, or visit our Web site: www.wish.org

Sincerely,

Paula Van Ness
President and CEO

Introduction

■

This is not your typical book. It doesn't have main characters, plots, or subplots. Nor are there protagonists confronting antagonists coming to some resolution in a climactic ending. This book is a collection of "favorite things" from the famous and not-so-famous; lists that are as varied as the individuals who wrote them. But if I had to name the one thing the letters do have in common, I could do so with a single word: *simplicity*. Whether the submission came from a former military general, a movie star, or a young child, all are celebrations of life's simple things.

Personally, if I were asked to write a submission for this book, I would not know where to end for fear of leaving something out. I would definitely include dinners with good friends and family that go well into the night; weekends at the Castle Hill Inn, in Newport, Rhode Island; the smell of bacon cooking on any morning; a James Taylor concert on a summer night; playing softball in Manhattan's Central Park or Chappaqua, NY; golden retrievers; *The New York Times* on Sunday; the sound of my goddaughter's voice; and all the ways my wife, Jackie, makes me smile. These are also simple things.

The idea for *These Are a Few of My Favorite Things* was born a few years ago when I had the pleasure of working with Bob Costas on a news segment for NBC television. After we worked together, I sent Bob a Christmas gift: a short book honoring Mickey Mantle. Within days, Bob returned a thoughtful note card in which he shared how much he appreciated my sentiment. His letter meant so much to me that I tacked it up on the bulletin board in my office. What amazed me was how my friends and colleagues reacted upon seeing the note. It was not the content they marveled at. Instead, they were fascinated to see his own stationery, his handwriting, and his signature up close and in person. Today, with e-mail, faxes, and telephone being so pervasive, the intimacy provided by a letter has been nearly lost. A handwritten letter has been physically touched, folded, and cared for before it reaches your mailbox. That is what drew my friends to open Bob's note card.

A portion of the proceeds from this book will be donated directly to the Make-A-Wish Foundation®. As a volunteer for the Foundation, I have experienced firsthand the sense of joy that this organization has bestowed upon others. The selflessness of the workers inspired me to bring greater recognition and financial support to their work through this book. As you share in the warmth of these letters, know that your purchase will help a child's wish come true. It is also my sincere hope that this collection will inspire you to remember your own favorite things. Jot them down and share them with loved ones.

Tony D. Burton

These Are a Few of My Favorite Things . . .

Bob Costas

These are a few of my favorite things:
   Baseball on the radio with Vin Scully...

Patsy's Pizza in Brooklyn....

A hot, soft, bagel, a steaming hot cup of joe
and The morning paper....

An Olympic feature in which people aren't crying...

These are a few of my
favorite things:

Opening Day
The Constitution
Bob Costas broadcasting
        baseball on radio
Cole Porter's songs
The Seventh Inning
        Stretch

Dry Martinis
Extra Innings

G. F. Will

1208 THIRTIETH STREET, N. W. · WASHINGTON, D. C. 20007

My favorite childhood memory is when I was 10 years old and I hit a homerun in my first Little League at-bat.

I enjoy listening to Bruce "The Boss" Springsteen who is also one of the most memorable people I have ever met!

A few of my favorite foods are a big juicy steak, pizza and chicken.

My favorite thing about being a father … EVERYTHING!

MARK McGWIRE

6615 EAST PACIFIC COAST HIGHWAY

SUITE 260

LONG BEACH, CALIFORNIA 90803

A few of my favorite things,

A nice calm lake for fishing and a cool day for playing tennis!

Hank Aaron

Doris Kearns Goodwin

These are a few of my favorite things:

Sitting at Fenway Park with my three sons, imagining myself back at Ebbets Field, a young girl once more in the presence of my father, watching the players of my youth on the grassy fields below — Jackie Robinson, Duke Snider, Pee Wee Reese.

Going to breakfast with my husband at the historic inn in the center of our town, knowing we've been married so long we can read the morning papers without feeling compelled to make conversation.

A roomful of books with a reading chair in the corner and a library ladder to reach the highest shelves.

Doris Kearns Goodwin

Late Night with Conan O'Brien

These are a few of my favorite
   things:

— canned baby peas

— <u>WW II</u> documentaries

— trying to get a gym sock away
from my dog

— days when my hair looks like
Jack Lord's from "Hawaii 5-0".

Conan O'Brien

CHEVY CHASE

These are a few
of my favorite
things:
- Birds.
- The smell of
Spring.
- Kicking around a
soccer ball.
- Playing Jazz Piano
- Listening to good
music
- Sharing all of these
things with my
three daugters!!!
XXX

[signature]

CARL REINER

There are a few of my
favorite things: -

- Eating a hot dog while
watching the Dodgers play.

- Going to a movie with
good friends.

- Playing silly games at a friend's house after dinner.
- Sitting at my computer and writing a new story.
- Visiting my three children and four grandchildren.
- Helping my wife cook dinner.
- Eating soup for breakfast.

Carl Reini

These are a few of my favorite things

My family. Yes even my brother Tom....
National Public Radio....
Father Timothy of Mitford North Carolina....
Not going to parties....
Watching classic movies....
Keeping fit and eating healthful food....
Being a straightman....
The Lord. For all of the challenges and
blessings He has placed in my life....

Dick Smothers

Gilbert Gottfried

A few of my favorite things:

1. An army of robots to do my bidding.

2. My picture on a $5 dollar bill.

3. A picture of me with my robots on a $10 dollar bill.

Gilbert Gottfried

Jennifer

■

Eleven-year-old Jennifer didn't have to think twice when volunteers from the Make-A-Wish Foundation® of Southern Nevada asked, "If you could have one wish, what would it be?" More than anything else, she wanted to meet her favorite television and film stars, the Olsen twins.

Since Jennifer was awaiting a kidney transplant, planning her wish was not an easy task. Yet, after rescheduling several times, volunteers were able to make Jennifer's dream a reality. She and her family went to California for a star-studded visit to the Olsen twins. She spent a day touring the studio and the set. More important, however, she was able to spend time with Ashley and Mary-Kate. As an added bonus, Jennifer hobnobbed with other Hollywood stars who crossed her path on the studio lot.

And as luck would have it, prior to the family's trip, a kidney donor was found—Jennifer's mother. Still reeling from the excitement and sheer magic of her wish come true, Jennifer entered the hospital with her mother and underwent a successful kidney transplant four days after meeting the Olsen twins.

Jennifer

Make-A-Wish Foundation®

these are a few
of my favorite things

Dolphins

horses

Beanie BaBies

Jump Roping

School

Music

Stuffed animals

BOB DOLE

There are
a few of my favorite things:

- - - - - - -

Sunday brunch with Elizabeth

Completing 30 minutes on
my treadmill

Watching T.V.--"Law & Order"

Making People laugh...

Eating chocolate ice cream -

Bob Dole

A few of my favorite things:

Snow skiing in New Hampshire

Enjoying North Carolina barbecue
with Bob

Reading a good book on a rainy
day

Walking along the Florida coast

Church on Easter Sunday

Elizabeth Dole

mary matalin
james carville

These are a few of my favorite things:

- The girls gurgling in a bubblebath, hugging & smooching, sandboxing, trampolining — just being

- Daddy enjoying his big screen tv

- good wine, food, company
- well written history books

Mary Matalin

mary matalin
james carville

These are a few of my favorite things:

1. The faces of my children when I see them after a business trip.

2. making a perfect Roux* — (only happens some of the time)

3. Hanging out with my wife.

*A roux is a mixture of flour and fat used to thicken sauces. Brown roux is basic to Cajun and Creole cooking.

RICHARD HOLBROOKE

These are a few of my favorite things —
Some are the small + personal pleasures of a private life;
Others are large and very important — the goals for which we live
— — — — — — — — — — — —

— Walking in the city — New York or Budapest — or on the
beach with my wife Kati;
— Skiing (in Telluride especially!) with my sons and
my step-children;

— a quiet evening with a few close friends;
— a quiet evening alone or alone with Kati;
— exploring ancient ruins off the beaten path;
  BUT ALSO:
— things that make a difference to other people —
  • helping to end a war, or prevent one;
  • organizing a refugee relief effort that saves lives;
  • teaching people that they must overcome racial
    or ethnic hatreds — concepts that plague our
    world even in the Age of the Internet.

Ben

■

Ben is a sixteen-year-old who wished for an in-line skating adventure. Volunteers for the Make-A-Wish Foundation® of Louisiana sent Ben and his family to California for the adventure of a lifetime. He had a marvelous time skating at the parks and practicing with a teen skate team. He even had a chance to meet a few skating pros!

Make-A-Wish Foundation®

Ben's top ten Favorites

1. Skating (Street)
2. music
3. Sufing the net
4. the beach
5. Playing the drums
6. food
7. Watching Skate videos
8. Watching basketball & football
9. hanging out at Skate park
10. Sleeping

— Ben

Waking up to sunshine makes me happy
As well as flowers, rainbows, & butterflies
A round of golf with good friends
And a good hug always brings a smile
I enjoy dancing to Janet & watching the
49ers win.
Hearing "I love you" from someone I love.
These, along with my friends & family
are just a few of my favorite things.

Kristi Yamaguchi

JIM NANTZ

These are a few of my favorite things—
A walk on a beach in Bermuda...
Taking my daughter to school...
The unharnessed joy of a child...
The Monterrey Peninsula...
The ceremonial tee shots, Thursday at the Masters...
Words...

©CBS SPORTS

Jim Nantz

My Favorite Things

MARVIN R. SHANKEN

- my wife, three daughters and grandson

- The pastrami "special" from Chuck's in New Haven, Connecticut

- A Hoyo de Monterrey Double Corona from Cuba

- A 1963 Graham Port or 61 Petrus

- A long nap on a Caribbean beach

Some of my favorite Things...
a hug from a loved one...
an idea I'd never heard...
an honest history or biography...
a great baseball game
a food piece of bread

Max Frankel

LETITIA BALDRIGE

A few of my favorite things:

Memories of how great I felt after three hours of tennis singles. (Why did I not properly appreciate my young joints?)

Peppermint stick ice-cream with hot fudge sauce and no calory worries

Visualizing myself lying on a Directoire sofa sipping champagne and re-reading every single Edith Wharton novel.

Giving a dinner party without a single glitch.

Seeing a young person for the first time in many years, and finding her no longer a brat, but grown-up, lovely, and "cool."

Gary Dell'Abate

* Watching a good Jets game on a cold Sunday afternoon, late in the season when they're still in contention (which rarely happens)
* Taking a swim in the quarry in Manchester, Vermont.
* A private party at SCORES
* Seeing my sons play together and getting along!

Gary Dell'Abate

Deborah

These are a few of my favorite things :
Great conversation ...
Liberace ...
Broadway shows ...
Home cooked Italian food ...
Lobster ...
Bowling (with my own ball !) ...
Finding new ways to hit a difficult high note ...
Romance ...
Billy Joel and Elton John ...
Dancing ...
Children ...

Deborah Gibson ♫

MICHAEL BOLTON

THESE ARE A FEW OF MY FAVORITE THINGS

MY THREE GIRLS

GOLF GOLF GOLF

SINGING FROM THE SOUL

SALLY'S PIZZA OF NEW HAVEN

FINALLY BEING AT PEACE AT HOME

AND LOVIE SWEET LOVIE

GRAND ILLUSION MUSIC©

Dennis DeYoung

6-4-99

1. Good health for myself, family and friends

2. My beautiful loving wife and two wonderful children.

3. Memorie of my father in his garden

4. My wifes marinara sauce.

5. Puccinis aria "Nessun dorma".

6. Watching the Beatles first performance on Ed Sullivan.

7. My peoples choice award for song of the year.

8. Vacationing in Italy.

9. My daughters business card for her own P.R. firm.

10. The moment I realize I've written a special song.

Denna Dey

15941 S. Harlem Ave., Suite 265 • Tinley Park, IL 60477

Kevin Sharp

■

Perhaps no one exemplifies the "power of a wish" more strongly than Kevin Sharp.

Kevin was referred to the Make-A-Wish Foundation® as a high-school senior in 1989. As an active teenager who loved singing and was planning a football career, Kevin was diagnosed with a rare form of bone cancer that had metastasized in his lungs. He was given only a 20 percent chance of living.

Kevin's wish was to meet record composer and producer David Foster, whose music had inspired Kevin throughout his life. Foster helped boost the careers of such musical legends as Barbra Streisand, Whitney Houston, and Natalie Cole. Kevin did indeed meet Foster. In the course of their conversation, Kevin indicated that he was interested in pursuing a musical career someday.

Over the next few years, Kevin defied everyone's expectations, except for his own, and he battled his cancer successfully into remission. He and Foster maintained a friendship throughout his recovery, and Foster soon came to find that Kevin was truly musically gifted.

Now, ten years later, Kevin, the former wish child, has become a country-music singing sensation. His signature song, "Nobody Knows," soared to number one on the *Billboard* country singles chart and remained there for four consecutive weeks. Shortly thereafter, his *Measure of a Man* album went platinum.

Kevin is special in another way. Because of his bout with cancer, Kevin feels a strong connection with other wish children. He enjoys sharing his story and his heart with children across the country who have life-threatening illnesses. He has granted more than a dozen wishes to children wanting to meet him; he meets with hundreds of wish children through special events and surprise hospital visits; he performs concerts to benefit the Make-A-Wish Foundation; and he serves as a PSA spokesperson for the Foundation. For his efforts, Kevin was presented with the Make-A-Wish Foundation Wish Granter of the Year Award in 1997.

Kevin, like many other wish children, credits the Make-A-Wish Foundation with helping to reinstill in him a sense of hope and optimism through a positive, life-affirming, and lifelong wish experience. Kevin received his wish—and he continues to live his dream.

KEVIN SHARP

THESE ARE A FEW OF MY FAVORITE
THINGS:

MY WIFES BLUE EYES.

A GOOD COUNTRY SONG.

WHEN A COMPLETE STRANGER SAYS
HELLO.

LOVE AND HOPE!

BEING ON STAGE!

THE MOVIE "RUDY"...

A BAKED POTATO...!

Paul

■

When volunteers from the Make-A-Wish Foundation® of Central New York met Paul, he was a thoughtful eighteen-year-old who wanted, more than anything, to attend the first game of the 1998 NBA playoffs between the Utah Jazz and the Chicago Bulls. His favorite team was the Jazz, and it was a thrill for him to watch them defeat the Bulls at home. To add to the excitement, he had the opportunity to meet many of the Jazz players. Paul was even given the game sneakers and sweatbands from Karl Malone!

Paul is no longer with us, but we are fortunate that he shared this poem with us. He teaches us that sometimes what you cherish most, what is truly your "favorite," is not necessarily "things," but the freedom to strive for your dreams, to hope, just to be.

Make-A-Wish Foundation®

Whatever you wish,
Whatever you dream,
Whatever you hope to achieve...
Whatever you try for,
Whatever you plan...
It is yours if you only believe.

Paul

Making movies
Playing Hockey
Jogging with my dogs
Sitting in a crowded
theater with "real people
eating popcorn and
watch a great movie with
my wife

OK here are a few:

Frank Sinatra & Nelson Riddle

Las Vegas

Thanksgiving dinner any day of the year

coconut layer cake

summer nights

Nora Ephron

NATIONAL
■ ACTORS ■
THEATRE

My favorite thing in the whole
world is my 23 mos old daughter
Julia saying to me each morning
when I go in with her bottle,
"Pick day up. Daddy."

Next comes Italian opera.

Tony Randall

Angela Lansbury

Here are a few of my favorite things.

Thanksgiving in New England...
Picking primroses & violets by the
roadside in the Spring in England...
The smell of an Irish Turf fire...
Canoeing alone on a lake at
                          sunset...
  Roast Chicken, gravy & mashed
                          potatoes...
  A baby's first smile...
The Art's & leisure section of the
                          N.Y. Times...

Angela Lansbury.

Teddy

■

Teddy loves planes. His favorite movie is *Top Gun*, and toy planes decorate his room. Despite this, his mother and father were shocked when Teddy enthusiastically proclaimed that he wanted to fly an F-14 as his wish. His family feared it would be too dangerous. But Teddy remained steadfast in his decision to fly an F-14, and thanks to volunteers from the Los Angeles Make-A-Wish Foundation® and representatives from Fighter Pilots U.S.A., his ultimate dream was possible.

When Teddy and his family arrived at the air base in Florida, Teddy attended flight-training school, which lasted for an hour. There he was briefed on the details of his upcoming mission. Then the most difficult part of his mission had to be accomplished—finding a flight suit small enough for Teddy's little body. With a few alterations (a couple of rolls of the pants legs here and there), Teddy had an official flight uniform to wear, complete with a helmet. To make the plane a perfect fit, a telephone book was provided for Teddy to sit on so that he could see above the dashboard to work the controls of the aircraft.

Then Teddy was off into the beautiful blue skies of sunny Florida. Teddy—a.k.a. "Mav"—performed loops, turned upside down, and emerged victorious from a simulated dog fight. He was quite proud when he received his wings and certificate of completion from his partner and teacher, Captain Wild. At the age of six, Teddy was the youngest person ever to go through the pilot program at Fighter Pilots U.S.A., in Kissimmee, Florida. He even took the videotape of his flight experience to school for his teacher and classmates to see, and he has informed everyone that he is going to be a fighter pilot when he grows up!

Make-A-Wish Foundation®

Teddy's favorite Stuff

1. Legos
2. F-14 Tomcat
3. Sleepy medicine for spinal taps
4. Computer games
5. Drawing

Teddy

These are a few of my favorite things:

Spending a nice quiet evening with
my wife Brooke...

Scuba diving...

A perfect meal followed by a great movie...

A Sunday drive around a race track
at about 190 m.p.h. ...

7100 Weddington Road ♥ Harrisburg, North Carolina 28075

DEEPAK CHOPRA

skiing, scuba diving,
meditation, reading, my family,
food, learning from the
creativity of children,
wonder, abandonment,
enthusiasm, inspiration
carefreeness, love

Deepak Chopra.

Vince McMahon

There are a few of my favorite things.

    Bull mastiffs

    protein bars

    working out

    brainstorming

    Raw is War

MISTER ROGERS' NEIGHBORHOOD

These are a few of my favorite things:

Children
Waves on the beach
Grandchildren
Yo-Yo Ma playing Bach
Susan Starr playing Bach
The Rogers-Morrison Duo playing Mozart
Simplicity
The Fox in "The Little Prince"
Silence
Thoughts of God's Faithful Love
Friends

These Are A Few of My FAVORITE
Things:
   My FAMily, including my
GRANdchildREN
   Getting good News on The
Telephone
   Snuggling into my wARM
Bed on A cold winter's
night.
   EATing chocolate
   Cooking Good Food AND
ShARing it with Those I
Love
                    Joyce Brothers

Florence Henderson

My Favorite Things

the love & respect of my husband & children & grandchildren

My brothers + sisters

Friends

My Work

Music   Boxing

Making people laugh

Sunsets

Looking up at the Sky

Italian Food

a delicious glass of Red Wine

Prayer

Life!

Living on a Boat with my Husband.

Margo

■

At the age of ten, Margo was a very bright student. However, her illness made her unable to attend school regularly. Her school loaned her a computer so she could stay in touch with her class, but Margo really wanted a computer of her own and a color printer.

Volunteers from the Make-A-Wish Foundation® of Western Pennsylvania were able to fulfil her wish. Margo enjoyed the computer games and used the computer to keep up with her classmates, but she also became very adept with the publishing programs that came with the system. Using her new tools and the color printer, she began to produce a monthly newsletter.

Margo is now fourteen years old and is an aspiring writer.

Make-A-Wish Foundation®

These Are A Few of my Favorite Things

- hanging out with my friends
- talking on the phone
- listening to music
- watching movies
- spending money
- having fun

-margo-

JOSEPH ABBOUD

These are a few of my FAVORITE Things —
A Baseball game at Fenway Park,
New England in October,
The Natural Rugged Beauty of Scotland,
Home by the Fire in a Snowstorm —
and a Long, Hard Hug from my Two
Daughters!

Joseph Abboud

BRYANT C. GUMBEL

These are a few of my favorite things —

The love of my children....
The lives of my friends,
The choices of freedom....
The challenge of golf,
The quiet of satisfaction....
The quality of life.

These are a few of my favorite things —
friends and family...
fall in New England...
Golf at anytime of year...
a trout stream in the rockies...
fine french food...
and sleeping past 4:00 AM!

Matt Lauer

These are a few of my favorite things...
Singing in the shower (or anyplace else!)
Bacon cooking on Sunday morning
Group hugs with my daughters
The beach at 5:00 p.m.
The way you feel after a shower
after a day at the beach
Cary Grant

Katie Couric

These are a few of my
favorite things...
    seeing my daughter's smile,
feeling my son's kisses,
holding my husband's hand,
and learning something new.

Ann Curry

Al Roker

These are a few of my
FAVORITE THINGS:

① The LOVE of MY TWO GIRLS.

② A BRIGHT, SUNNY DAY.

③ SMILES FROM THE PEOPLE I
MEET!

Al Roker

Kelsey

■

Volunteers from the Make-A-Wish Foundation® of Western Pennsylvania arranged Kelsey's wish to experience a cruise with the magical touches of a world-famous theme park in Orlando, Florida. No words could describe the look on six-year-old Kelsey's face as she and her family drove toward Port Canaveral in Florida and she saw the cruise ship in the distance. Docked peacefully in the harbor, the cruise ship, one of the two ships of the Southern Florida cruise line, took Kelsey and her family on the trip of a lifetime.

As part of the cruise package, Kelsey and her family also enjoyed a visit to the theme park and a stay at a beautiful hotel, where a kind employee gave Kelsey bean-bag toys of the theme park's characters to make sure her room was properly decorated with the images of her mouse couple.

While on board the ship, Kelsey spent a great deal of her time in the pool. Her favorite activity was riding the slide from the tenth deck of the ship down to the pool on the ninth deck.

Make-A-Wish Foundation®

My favorite
things are:
1. helping Dad
2. hugs from Mom
3. hot dogs
4. Playing with my sister
5. sleeping at Grammy and

Pappy's house
6. My stuffed Animal
   named Puppy-puppy
7. My blankie

Kelsey

NBC NEWS

These are a few of
my favorite things —

A baby's smile.

grandpa's laugh.

spicy pasta.

crisp, sunny mornings.

spring training with
my son.

Tim Russert

These are a few of my
favorite things....

- cuddling with my husband
- laughing with my kids
- playing with my kids
- Hanging out with my 4
  Brothers
- teasing and talking with my
  Parents
- fighting with my bosses 😊
- gabbing with my girlfriends

- lying on a massage
  table on the beach in
  Maui !!

STONE S. PHILLIPS

These are a few of my favorite things:

Yellow Labs
Coaching Little League Baseball
Fast Cars
My Wife's Killer Forehand
Pick-up Basketball
Long TD Passes

Stone Phillips

FAVORITE THINGS:

1.   *My family, most of all*

2.   *Sage and Abbie, our two wonder dogs*

3.   *Fly rods*

JOHN F. WELCH
3135 EASTON TURNPIKE
FAIRFIELD, CT 06431

These are a few of my favorite things:

- Hanging out in Nantucket in August.
- Playing golf --- almost anywhere.
- Eating pasta with friends on Friday night.
- Being at GE's learning center with employees.

Jack Welch

These are a few of my favorite
things:

A Texas Ranger baseball
game with my family

Bass Fishing

PANCAKES

Jogging on Town Lake
in Austin

Mexican Food with
friends

Hugs from my Daughters

Robert

∎

More than anything, Robert wanted to visit the world-famous theme park in Orlando, Florida, and meet his favorite character, Goofy. The volunteers with the Make-A-Wish Foundation® of Metro New York were happy to oblige. As Robert's trip to Walt Disney World approached, the three-year-old with congenital heart disease became quite ill. His doctors didn't know if he would pull along, but they thought days filled with fun, warm weather, and sunshine could be just the cure for a child who had been bedridden for fourteen consecutive days.

Robert had to be carried or wheeled around because he was so weak, and after becoming very sick on the plane ride, he spent a restless first night in Florida. His parents, Charlene and Irwin, considered returning to New York the next morning, but a snowstorm up north prevented that. Later that morning, Goofy sent a big plate of chocolate strawberries with an autographed picture to Robert's hotel room. Soon after, Robert ate lunch with many of the characters that inhabited the park. He ate some bacon and potato chips. And he loved the ice-cream bar, which was shaped like the famous mouse cartoon character. It was the first solid food he had eaten in weeks.

Slowly Robert began to feel better. He loved attending the shows, going on the rides, and seeing all the characters walking around the park. The trip was a total revival for him. Today, he still battles his illness, but the memories of his trip will always be with him. A wall in his room is dedicated to the Make-A-Wish Foundation, with photos and souvenirs from the trip.

I LIKE DRAGONS

AND DINOSAYRS

ROBERT

HELEN THOMAS

FRONT ROW AT THE WHITE HOUSE

MY LIFE AND TIMES

With all best wishes.

Helen Thomas

These are a few
of my favorite
things:

1. Handling a
big breaking
story.

2. Sitting in an outdoor cafe and watching the world roll by.

3. Travel on Air Force One

4. Conversation at midnight with friends.

5 Christmas

6. Beautiful music

7. Arabic food

8. Learning about everything

JAMES A. BAKER, III
ONE SHELL PLAZA
910 LOUISIANA
HOUSTON, TEXAS 77002-4995

These are a few of my favorite things.

a Wyoming trout stream in summer
a high mountain meadow in fall
a South Texas ranch in winter
a southern state golf course in spring

James A. Baker III

PATRICK J. BUCHANAN   Feb. 22/99

A few of my Favorite Things are:
Going Through old book store for American History
& Diplomacy volumes, Shelley's spaghetti on Sunday evening,
Vacation days on The "Eastern Shore" of Md & Delaware,
The old Latin Mass on Sundays at St. Mary's, and
Reunions with The Guys I grew up with.

Pat Buchanan

MUTUAL OF OMAHA'S
WILDLIFE HERITAGE CENTER

With so many things to enjoy in life
Its difficult to make a list.... but here
goes!! -

- Traveling to the wildest places on
earth to study, film and observe
wildlife.

- Traveling anywhere with my wife
and two children, camping, hiking,
going on safari

- working on old cars and tractors

- Presenting live animals before audiences
such as the Explorer's Club annual
dinner — in the ballroom of the Waldorf
Astoria.

- and of course... wrestling crocodiles
and anacondas!

Jim Fowler

"TODAY SHOW"
WILDLIFE CORRESPONDENT

Christmas in Buffalo with my family
Announcing an NFL Game on any
given Sunday.
Fried oysters at the beach in Charleston
18 holes of golf and winning 1-up.
Chili Rellenos and a cold "Bud"
PAUL L MAGUIRE   Paul Maguire

PHIL SIMMS

Things I Really Like

Chocolate
Italian food with lots of garlic.

Watching and helping my
kids grow up with my wife.
But most of all Kindness and
compassion people show to each
other.

Phil Simms

P.S. - Golf.

These are a few of
my favorite things.

1. A litter of fluffy Labrador puppies
2. Alaskan Hunting & Fishing Trips.
3. Fall in Ohio
4. 1930 model "A" pick up trucks
5. Brand new chain saw for firewood
6. Sitting around a camp fire with
   family & friends anywhere!
7. Old, "Friends hunting dogs!

Larry Csonka

Tracy Austin

These are a few of my favorite things...

★ playing games with my children...
★ a long hike in the mountains with friends...
★ a quiet dinner with my husband —
    ceasar salad, steak and baked potato...
★ a good book on a lazy afternoon...
★ planting flowers in the spring....

Tracy Austin

Joe Garagiola

These are a few of my favorite things

The expression on the face of a youngster, especially one of my grandchildren, when they get a present. The Christmas look is always best because they have been asking Santa Claus for a particular gift - then they get it.

The smell of a brand new car.

The look, the confidence, the feeling of accomplishment when a deadly, addictive habit is broken, be it drugs, alcohol or tobacco.

The aroma of risotto and then the taste because
it reminds me of our Sunday dinner when I was
growing up.

The voice of Luciano Pavarotti or Andrea Bocelli
singing a song my father used to sing.

The kids at St Peter Indian Mission in
Arizona (Pima Indians), especially the kindergarten,
singing in church to the Great Spirit

The optimism of the sandlot or Little League
youngster during a baseball game. You just
can't top, "C'mon guys, we need only 15
runs to tie 'em".

Rolando

∎

   Rolando's mother works for the fire department, and many of the firefighters spend time skiing and snowboarding. Rolando is very close to all the firefighters and loves to listen to them talk about their snowboarding adventures. He had always dreamed of participating in the fun, but he never believed it would be possible.

   Rolando has a condition that prevents him from enjoying the outdoors. His sensitive skin must always be protected from the sun. So when volunteers from the Make-A-Wish Foundation® of Southern Florida asked Rolando, "If you could have one wish, what would it be?" Rolando shared his wish to go snowboarding. However, he said he would settle for a computer, since he believed his condition would keep his wish from coming true.

   Immediately, the volunteers accepted the challenge and set off to make Rolando's snowboarding dream a reality. With the assistance of the Make-A-Wish Foundation of Northeast New York, Rolando was able to attend the world-class snowboarding school in Lake Placid, New York. There he spent a miraculous day on the slopes with his family and his favorite instructor, Dave. Now Rolando can declare, from firsthand experience, that snowboarding is one of his favorite things.

Make-A-Wish Foundation®

Dave

me

my wish to go snowbor=ding came
true in Lake Placid Ny

Rolando age 11

These are a few of my favourite things.

NEIL SIMON

1) Morning
2) The Sports Pages
3) Speaking on the phone with my daughters.
4) Seeing a good play.
5) Writing a good play.
6) Feeling Healthy.
7) Being Healthy.
8) Seeing the face of someone I love.
9) Almost any Humphrey Bogart movie.
10) Laughing until it hurts.
11) Crying when its the only release to
    retieve a pain.
12) Good art, any period, any style.
13) Being in love.
14) A Good nights sleep.
15) Another morning.

ROBERT KLEIN

A few of my favorite things;
(not necessarily in order)

1. My son Allie
   laughter
   Good deeds — courage and honesty
   Watching the Yankees, Knicks, Giants
   and Jets
   the New York Times
   W. C. Fields

Robert Klein

brian dennehy

1 — Being with my kids —
2 — Being with my grandchildren —
3 — Working on my farm in Connecticut
4 — Sailing —
5 — Being with my kids —

Brian Dennehy

These are a few of my favorite things:

- Christmas Eve
- Snow on my birthday
- puppy dogs
- spaghetti and meatballs
- hot fudge sundaes
- fire in the fireplace
- Spring
- Dancing

Susan Lucci

Brett Butler

These are a few of my favorite things:

My relationship with God the Father —

The beauty of my wife and my children's love —

The sound of waves crashing on the beach at night —

Baseball anytime - anyplace —

The support of friends in tough times —

and sleeping in til 10:00 —

Brett Butler

MIAMI
HEAT

These ARE A few of my
FAVORite Things—

— Spend Time with my Kids As much
As possible...

— Going out with my family AND FRiends
To parties...

— I Love fried Chicken + Spaghetti AND
Some bread...

— I Like watching Sitcoms with my
wife at Home...

signature

Amanda

■

    Seven-year-old Amanda wished for her very own playhouse, someplace she could go to play with her friends or spend time alone. And she wanted a place equipped with all the amenities a child could dream of. Volunteers for the Los Angeles Make-A-Wish Foundation® were happy to oblige. Amanda received a custom-built playhouse with a slide, swing, sky tower, and cargo net. She immediately fell in love with her "dream house" and placed a chair in it. She likes to sit and read to her dolls.

Make-A-Wish Foundation®

rollerblading
coloring
playing Games
Watching T.V.

these Are a
few of my favorite
things

Amanda

BOB VILA

SOME OF MY FAVORITE THINGS

WAKING UP AT HOME ON A WARM SPRING
MORNING AND STAYING THERE.

CHRISTMAS MORNING WITH THE KIDS.

GOING OUT FOR AN AFTERNOON SAIL
JUST WITH MY WIFE.

TRAVELING TO AN ANCIENT CITY.

MAKING A SIMPLE DINNER AT HOME
WITH WIFE & SHARING A GREAT WINE

Bob Vila

These are a few of my favorite things:

Yoga!!!

Sitting around a big table with all of my friends eating a wonderful meal and just enjoying conversation and good food!

A crackling fire on a cold night!

Sipping a big mug of tea in front of the crackling fire.

New York City in every season!

Anything french!

My favorite things are quite simple, you see,
Tulips in Springtime & Sailboats at Sea
All parts of a baby; it's Bottom, it's toes —
And the sweet little nostrils on it's sweet little nose
I love the Sun when it Dawns, & right after,
Old fences with roses, & Kindness, & Laughter
The skip of a child, the Song of a lark,

Saturdays an Sundays an Walks in a Park.
Prayertime an Lunchtime an time by Myself,
Crying at Movies, Old Books on a Shelf.
Clean, crisp sheets on a freshly made Bed;
Watching a race when a friend is ahead.
Fires in Wintertime, Apples in Autumn,
Wearing New clothes right after I've bought 'em.
Feeling much better when I've been sick
long-lasting hugs an lilacs just picked.

The smell of a baby right after you bathe it
My husband's face, right after he shaves it.
Window boxes with Life overflowing
Rocking horses on soft breezes blowing.
"The simpler, the better" is my motto, I guess
Knowing God loves me is the thing I like best.

Kathie Lee

Dear Martin records, Joe Di Maggio stories, Columbus Avenue in Manhattan, Notre Dame campus, New York Skyline

Regis Philbin

C. Everett Koop, M.D.

seeing a disabled person achieve
a goal
feeling the dusk begin to fall
sailing with gunwale awash
listening to the Hallelujah Chorus.

C. Everett Koop

Geraldine A. Ferraro

These are a few of my favorite things —

My 2½ year old granddaughter calling me
her girl friend

Being with my family

Phone calls from my grandchildren

My garden in the Spring.

A good book on a rainy day.

Swimming laps in a heated pool

A plate of ziti with homemade marinara sauce

Doing something that impacts positively on
peoples' lives —

Geraldine A. Ferraro

Buzz Aldrin
Astronaut

These are a few of my favorite things...

...a trip to the moon on our Eagle's wing

...a dive to the deep — sharks, eels and Titanic hulls

...ice breaker treks to polar bears and penguin's poles

...to share space with you, the new tourists in orbit

...and, a trip to Mars on the Aldrin Space Cycler!

T Buzz Aldrin

AMERICA'S PROMISE
THE ALLIANCE FOR YOUTH™

FAVORITE THINGS

— FAMILY ABOVE ALL

— ALL KIDS

— A NYC CORNER HOT DOG
WITH RED ONIONS,

General Colin L. Powell, USA (Ret)
Chairman

April

■

For a senior in high school, one of the most important pastimes is shopping. When volunteers from the Make-A-Wish Foundation® of Oklahoma asked April what her one wish would be, she told them she wanted a shopping spree. She really wanted to buy a prom dress, a leather jacket, and new makeup. April got all of those things, plus a make-over, limousine ride, and a night on the town.

Going to the mall with some of my friends.
Talking and shopping til day never ends.

Being with my sister and having girl talk.
Taking my dog, Winston, for a walk.

Sitting with my parents on a cold winter night,
by the fireplace warm with sparkles so bright.

Going to my grandparents on a holiday..
Watching my cousins as they laugh and play.

Holding my nephew with his brown eyes...
Making me laugh, he never cries.

Singing with the radio when I feel really good.
Driving my car when my Dad said I could.

Going on a trip from coast to coast...
These are some of the things I enjoy most.

April
Age 18

R.L. Stine

* WRITING THE <u>LAST</u> SENTENCE OF A BOOK.

* OLD <u>BOB</u> & <u>RAY</u> TAPES

* DOG LICKS

* FAN MAIL THAT BEGINS: "OUR TEACHER IS FORCING US TO WRITE TO YOU..."

* CENTRAL PARK ON ANY SUNDAY MORNING

YOGI BERRA

I hope and dream everyone
has something to look forward to.

Yogi.

(Sung to the tune of "My Favorite Things")

Riding my bike and a cup of espresso
Coaching my kids while they're playing
                                    Nintendo
Ethel Merman when a "Silent Night" sings
These are a few of my favorite things

Weekends with family where we get to sleep
                                    in late
Enjoying a really long hot Philly cheese
                                    steak

Feeling the warmth that my wife's laughter
These are a few of my favorite things

When reviews suck
Then a films tanks
Ticket sales go bad
I simply remember my favorite things
And then I don't feel so bad

John Williams

Contributors' Index

Henry L. "Hank" Aaron enjoyed a twenty-three-year major-league career, during which he rewrote baseball's hitting record book. He holds more major-league batting records than any other player in the game's history, including the most home runs, lifetime, 755 and most runs batted in, lifetime, 2297. On May 17, 1970, Aaron became the first player to compile both 3,000 career hits and more than 500 homers. Aaron was inducted into the Baseball Hall of Fame at Cooperstown, New York, on August 1, 1982.

Joseph Abboud is a noted clothing designer. He received the men's knitwear design award from Woolknit Associates in 1986, the Cutty Sark Award as most promising menswear designer in 1987, the Woolmark award as best designer of menswear in 1988; and was named the 1989–90 Menswear Designer of the year by Council Fashion Designers of America.

Buzz Aldrin, along with crewmate Neil Armstrong, made history on July 20, 1969, as they took humankind's first steps on the Moon. Aldrin is a leading voice in charting the course of future space efforts, chairing both the National Space Society and the ShareSpace Foundation.

Tracy Austin won the U.S. Open women's singles championships in 1979 at the age of sixteen, becoming the youngest player ever to do so. She won again two years later, in 1981. Austin piled up 29 career singles titles in a professional career that spanned from 1977–94. At the age of twenty-nine years and seven months, she was the youngest inductee into the International Tennis Hall of Fame (1992).

James A. Baker, III, served as the sixty-first Secretary of State. He also served as Secretary of the Treasury from 1985–88 for the Reagan administration. He is currently honorary chairman of the Baker Institute, and a member of the Rice University Board of Governors.

Letitia Baldridge was chief of staff for Jacqueline Kennedy, and White House social secretary from 1961–63. She is the author of numerous books on etiquette, including *Amy Vanderbilt's Everyday Etiquette.*

Yogi Berra spent nineteen years in the major leagues, and he played all but four games of his career in New York Yankee pinstripes. The three-time MVP (1951, 1954, 1955) was not only famous as a power-hitting, lefty-swinging catcher, but also as a lovable figure with a knack for voicing humorous quotes that still bring the house down. (Among them: "We made too many wrong mistakes," "The other team could make trouble for us if they win," and the always popular "It's déjà vu all over again" and "It gets late early out here.")

Michael Bolton, a pop-music artist known for his soulful ballads, achieved superstar status in 1989 after the release of his fourth album, *Soul Provider,* which generated five Top 40 singles, including the Grammy Award–winning "How Am I Supposed to Live Without You?" He released *Timeless,* a collection of cover songs, in 1992; and *My Secret Passion,* an album of opera arias, in 1998.

Tom Brokaw is a well-respected television journalist whose popularity with American viewers grew during his term as host of the *Today* show (1976–81). Since 1983, he has been anchor and managing editor of *NBC Nightly News with Tom Brokaw.*

Joyce Brothers, Ph.D., first gained national attention as a quiz-show celebrity in the 1950s, winning the big prize on both *The $64,000 Question* and *The $64,000 Challenge.* She was a co-host of NBC Television's *Sports Showcase,* then appeared in a series of different syndicated television programs as a psychologist. She currently writes a daily syndicated newspaper column and several monthly magazine columns.

Jerry Bruckheimer is one of the most successful movie producers of all time. His many blockbuster films include *Flashdance,* the *Beverly Hills Cop* movies, *Top Gun, Bad Boys, Dangerous Minds, Crimson Tide, The Rock, Con Air,* and *Armegeddon.* His films have produced worldwide revenues of more than $3.5 billion in box office, video, and recording receipts, more than any other producer in history.

Patrick J. Buchanan has been a senior adviser to three presidents and twice been a candidate for the Republican presidential nomination.

George W. Bush is the forty-sixth governor of Texas. He began his career in the oil and gas business in Midland in 1975, and he worked in the energy industry until 1986. In 1989, he and a group of partners purchased the Texas Rangers baseball franchise and later built the Rangers's new home, the Ballpark at Arlington.

Brett Butler is considered by many as the prototype leadoff hitter in baseball. During his sixteen years in the major leagues, Butler has compiled a .291 batting average with 2,278 hits, 1,307 runs, and 544 stolen bases. Off the field, Butler is heavily involved with both the Los Angeles and Atlanta communities.

James Carville, campaign strategist for the Democratic Party, is the author of several best-sellers, including *We're Right, They're Wrong,* and coauthor, with his wife, Mary Matalin, of *All's Fair.*

Chevy Chase joined the *Saturday Night Live* crew in 1975 and amused audiences with his deadpan humor and outrageous stunts. A role opposite Goldie Hawn in *Seems Like Old Times* (1980) brought success to him on the big screen. Chase went on to score several comedy hits in the eighties with *Caddyshack* (1980), the National Lampoon's *Vacation* (1983) and *Fletch* (1985).

Deepak Chopra is the bestselling author of several alternative-healing books, including *Ageless Body, Timeless Mind* (1993) and *The Seven Spiritual Laws of Success* (1995), which combine herbal remedies, meditation, massage, and yoga.

Bob Costas joined NBC Television in 1980 and has since hosted just about every major sporting event, including numerous World Series, Super Bowls, NBA championships, and, most notably, the 1992 summer Olympics in Barcelona.

Katie Couric is a popular and respected morning news-show host. She has been coanchor of NBC's *Today* show since 1991.

Larry Csonka was the Miami Dolphins's first-round draft pick in 1968. He charged so tenaciously through defenses that his nickname, Zonk, became a new American verb. From 1971–73, he led the Dolphins to three Super Bowl appearances, earning All-Pro and Pro Bowl honors along the way.

Ann Curry, a four-time winner of the Golden Mike Award, is currently the news anchor on NBC's *Today* show.

Gary Dell'Abate has been the producer of *The Howard Stern Radio Show* for the past fourteen years. He is also known on-air as "Boy Gary" or "Baba Booey."

Brian Dennehy, a burly actor often cast as a tough guy or villain, began appearing in movies in the late 1970s. His film credits include *Semi-Tough* (1977), *Silverado* (1985), *F/X* (1986), *Presumed Innocent* (1990), and *Romeo and Juliet* (1996). In 1999, he received a Tony Award for his work in *Death of a Salesman*.

Dennis DeYoung was lead vocalist for Styx, one of the most successful stadium rock bands of the 1970s, and the first group ever to have four consecutive triple-platinum albums. In the summer of 1996, STYX reunited for the first time in thirteen years to tour the United States, much to the delight of its loyal fans, who flocked to the shows, making the Return to the Paradise Theatre tour one of that summer's most successful concerts—financially and critically. In 1994, DeYoung resumed his solo career, recording an album devoted to one of his true loves—show tunes.

Elizabeth Dole has had a remarkable public service career. In 1971, she was appointed Deputy Assistant to President Nixon for Consumer Affairs. In February 1983, Mrs. Dole joined President Reagan's cabinet as Secretary of Transportation—the first woman to hold that position. She was sworn in by President George Bush as the nation's twentieth Secretary of Labor in January 1989. As President of the American Red Cross, the world's foremost humanitarian organization, from 1991–99, Mrs. Dole oversaw more than 30,700 paid employees and 1.3 million volunteer staff members. She is married to Robert Dole.

Robert Joseph Dole, political leader and statesman, was born in Russell, Kansas, on July 22, 1923. After serving five and a half years in World War II in the U.S. Army, Dole was elected to the Kansas legislature in 1950, and he served in the House of Representatives from 1951–53. In 1960, Dole was elected to the U.S. House of Representatives; he was reelected in 1962, 1964, and 1966. He was elected to the U.S. Senate in 1968; he was re-elected in 1974, 1980, 1986, and 1992. In 1984, he was elected Senate majority leader, and thereafter served four consecutive Congresses as Senate Republican leader, until he retired from the Senate in 1996 to seek the GOP nomination for the Presidency.

Nora Ephron, screenwriter, director, and actress, is noted particularly for her screenplays that feature strong female leads. She earned Academy Award nominations for Best Screenplay for *Silkwood* (1983) and *When Harry Met Sally* (1989). She wrote and directed *This Is My Life* (1992), *Sleepless in Seattle* (1993), and *You've Got Mail* (1998).

Geraldine A. Ferraro served three terms in the U.S. House of Representatives (1979–84). In 1984, as Walter Mondale's running mate, she became the first woman nominated for the Vice-Presidency by a major political party in the United States.

Jim Fowler is the host of Mutual of Omaha's *Wild Kingdom* and serves as executive director of Mutual of Omaha's Wildlife Heritage Center.

Max Frankel writes a biweekly column on communications for *The New York Times Magazine*. He is a former executive editor of the *Times*, and he has also been editor of the paper's editorial pages. Mr. Frankel was chief Washington correspondent and head of the Washington bureau from 1968–73, Sunday editor until 1976, editor of the editorial page from 1977–86, and executive editor from 1986–94. He won a Pulitzer Prize in 1973 for his reporting of President Nixon's visit to China the previous year.

Joe Garagiola played for the Cardinals in five seasons, including the 1946 championship year. After his pro career ended in 1954, he joined St. Louis radio station KMOX and broadcast Cardinals games the next year. After moving to the Yankees, Garagiola called baseball for NBC television for twenty-seven years. Two stints with the *Today* show capped his illustrious broadcasting career. A 1973 winner of television's Peabody Award, Joe Garagiola entered the broadcasters' wing of the Baseball Hall of Fame in 1991.

Deborah Gibson got her first recording contract at age sixteen, for a twelve-inch aimed at the dance market. In late 1986, "Only in My Dreams" was released. Her first album, titled *Out of the Blue*, went triple platinum, just like her second album, *Electric Youth*, which was released in January 1989. With the song "Foolish Beat," she set a record—she became the youngest artist in chart history to have written, produced, and performed a number-one song.

Kathie Lee Gifford was originally a gospel singer, and is now best known for her morning television show, *Live with Regis and Kathie Lee.* She is married to sports commentator Frank Gifford.

Doris Kearns Goodwin received the 1995 Pulitzer Prize for History for her groundbreaking work *No Ordinary Time: Franklin and Eleanor Roosevelt: The Home Front During World War II.* She is also the author of *The Fitzgeralds and Kennedys* and *Lyndon Johnson and the American Dream.* All three books spent numerous weeks on *The New York Times* bestseller list. She has also written many articles on politics and baseball for dozens of leading national publications.

Jeff Gordon is the youngest NASCAR Winston Cup Series champion in the modern era, having achieved that distinction at age twenty-four in 1995. He was the youngest title-holder since Bill Rexford won the title at age twenty-three in 1950. His three championships and forty wins in a four-year span put him in the same league with some of the true immortals in the sport's history.

Gilbert Gottfried began his career performing stand-up comedy in his native New York before he joined the cast of *Saturday Night Live* for one season (1980–81). He has since gone on to appear in a number of features and television specials. His distinctive shrill voice has been used effectively for several animated features, most notably in the role of Iago the evil parrot in the Disney hit *Aladdin.*

Bryant C. Gumbel hosted NBC Television's *Today* show from 1982–97. Before joining *Today*, he hosted NBC's *NFL '81*. He is currently coanchoring *The Early Show* on CBS Television.

Tim Hardaway has been the Miami Heat's stellar point guard since February 1996.

Florence Henderson is perhaps best known for her role as Carol Brady on the television series *The Brady Bunch*, which aired from 1969–74, and has been shown in 122 countries around the world. She is currently cohost of NBC Television's *Later Today*.

Richard Holbrooke, who negotiated an accord with Slobodan Milosevic in 1998 for international supervision of Serbian forces' withdrawal from Kosovo, was appointed the United States ambassador to the United Nations in 1999.

Robert Klein is a veteran of Chicago's famous Second City comedy troupe. Klein has appeared on the *Ed Sullivan Show, Johnny Carson's Tonight Show, Late Night with David Letterman, Saturday Night Live* (he was part of the original "cheeseburger, cheeseburger" skit with Dan Akroyd and the late John Belushi), *Tom Snyder's Late Show*, and five "one-man" HBO comedy specials.

C. Everett Koop, M.D., was Surgeon General of the United States from 1981–89. He simultaneously supervised the activities of the Public Health Service Commission and offered counsel on essential health issues, including AIDS, smoking, alcohol abuse, environmental hazards, diet, and nutrition. He currently serves as Senior Scholar at the C. Everett Koop Institute at Dartmouth, and as the Elizabeth DeCamp McInerny Professor of Medical Ethics at Dartmouth's medical school.

Angela Lansbury is the Tony Award–winning stage, film, and television actress best known for her role as crime-solver Jessica Fletcher on television's *Murder, She Wrote* (1984–96). She has also had great success in plays and films.

Plays in which she starred include *Mame* (1966) and *Gypsy* (1975). Her films include *The Manchurian Candidate* (1962) and *The Pirates of Penzance* (1983).

Matt Lauer became coanchor of NBC Television's popular *Today* show on January 6, 1997.

Susan Lucci has starred for more than thirty years as Erica Kane, the dazzling femme fatale on the ABC Television Network's Emmy Award–winning daytime series *All My Children*. Ms. Lucci was honored in 1999 with the Emmy Award as Outstanding Actress in a Daytime Drama Series after being nominated for the award nineteen times.

Paul Maguire played professional football for eleven years as a punter and linebacker with the San Diego Chargers (1960–63) and the Buffalo Bills (1964–70), winning AFL championships in 1963, 1964, and 1965. He holds Buffalo's punting record for longest-season average (42.1 yards per kick), and was named to the Bills' Silver Anniversary All-Time Team as a punter in 1984.

Julianna Margulies is an Emmy Award–winning television and film actress. She's best known for her role as Nurse Carol Hathaway in the TV hospital drama *ER*.

Mary Matalin is a current-events talk-show host and former deputy campaign manager for President Bush. She is the wife of legendary campaign strategist James Carville, with whom she coauthored the bestselling political campaign book *All's Fair: Love, War, and Running for President*.

Mark McGwire inspired a renaissance of America's "national pastime" as he blasted his way to a major-league record 70 home runs, eclipsing Roger Maris's 1961 record of 61 homers.

Vincent K. McMahon bought his father's wrestling company, the Capitol Wrestling Corporation, in 1982. He then set out to realize the vision known today as the World Wrestling Federation, which attracts half a billion global viewers each week, in addition to garnering enormous live-event success.

Jim Nantz, the voice of CBS Sports, was named lead play-by-play announcer for college basketball in 1990, and has called regular season and NCAA Division I Men's Basketball Championship coverage since then. Nantz also serves as the lead play-by-play announcer for the U.S. Open tennis championships. He has handled play-by-play at the U.S. Open for eight years overall.

Conan O'Brien replaced David Letterman as the host of *Late Night* at NBC Television in 1993. Before taking over the popular talk show, O'Brien wrote for *The Simpsons* and *Saturday Night Live,* the latter of which won him an Emmy Award.

Regis Philbin, in a career spanning thirty-five years, has enjoyed more successes with more talk shows than possibly any other individual on television. In 1983, Philbin returned to his native Manhattan and created *The Morning Show* on WABC-TV. He was joined by Kathie Lee Gifford in June 1985, and the chemistry of their vinegar-and-honey personalities sent the ratings soaring. In September 1988, when *The Morning Show* debuted in national syndication, the title was changed to *LIVE with Regis & Kathie Lee.* Philbin has been Emmy Award–nominated seven times for his cohosting effort.

Stone S. Phillips is a principal anchor of the Emmy Award–winning *Dateline NBC.* Before joining the NBC Television News, he had been a correspondent for *20/20* since 1986, filing more than 100 reports on a wide variety of subjects.

General Colin L. Powell U.S.A. (Ret.) is the author of his bestselling autobiography, *My American Journey,* which traces his life from his birth to immigrant Jamaican parents in Harlem, to his role in advising this country's three most recent chief executives, presidents Reagan, Bush, and Clinton. General Powell was a professional soldier for thirty-five years, during which time he held a myriad of command and staff positions. Since 1997, he has been serving as chairman of America's Promise—The Alliance for Youth, the national crusade aimed at producing a significant nationwide increase in positive youth development support for all children who need help.

Tony Randall has appeared in well over a dozen films, but it wasn't until *The Odd Couple* that he attained widespread fame. In 1975, he won an Emmy for his performance on the television show. In 1991, Randall finally accomplished what had been a dream of his for decades, when he established the National Actor's Theater, which presents revivals of classic plays at affordable prices. He is the executive producer of the company and has performed in some of its plays.

Carl Reiner is an Emmy Award–winning actor, writer, and director, considered one of television's most creative minds. His credits include *Caesar's Hour* (1954–57) and *The Dick Van Dyke Show* (1961–66), for which he wrote, produced, and played the role of Alan Brady. He directed the films *Oh, God!* (1977) and *The Jerk* (1979). His son is actor-director Rob Reiner.

Mr. Rogers has received numerous awards from the television industry and from pro-family organizations since his program began in 1968. He has received several Emmy awards, two Lifetime Achievement awards, and two George Foster Peabody awards.

Al Roker is the weather and feature reporter on the NBC Television News show *Today*.

Tim Russert is the moderator of *Meet the Press*, and political analyst for *NBC Nightly News* and *Today*. He anchors *The Tim Russert Show*, a weekly program on CNBC that examines the role of the media in American society.

Marvin R. Shanken has built what many consider to be one of the world's most influential groups of lifestyle publications by sharing his personal pleasures with readers around the globe. His company, M. Shanken Communications, produces *Impact*, *Wine Spectator*, and *Cigar Aficionado* magazines, among others.

Maria Shriver is a contributing anchor for *Dateline NBC* and author of the bestselling *What's Heaven*. Shriver also anchors *First Person with Maria Shriver*, a series of NBC Television News prime-time specials. The program was honored with a first-place Commendation Award from American Women in Radio and Television. She is married to Arnold Schwarzenegger.

Phil Simms, Super Bowl XXI MVP and a fifteen-year NFL veteran, joined CBS Sports in January 1998 as lead analyst for coverage of the NFL on CBS. As an All-Pro quarterback, Simms led the New York Giants to two Super Bowl titles.

Neil Simon is a Pulitzer Prize– and Tony Award–winning playwright known for his popular plays about middle-class America that often touch on sex, marriage, and middle age. His plays include *Barefoot in the Park* (1963), *The Odd Couple* (1965), *Brighton Beach Memoirs* (1983), and *Lost in Yonkers* (1991).

Dick Smothers and his brother, Tom, have entertained audiences for more than three and a half decades. They had their own prime-time comedy series in both the 1960s and 1980s. The brothers have also done guest appearances on numerous television programs and talk shows, countless engagements as headliners in Las Vegas, a hot-selling video, continuous coast-to-coast concert tours, and a host of other accomplishments. In Hollywood, the entertainment world distinguished them with a star on the noted Walk of Fame.

Robert Lawrence Stine, who started writing stories when he was nine years old, is the author of the popular Goosebumps® book series. His fans, children aged seven to eleven (and their teachers and parents), have been gobbling up his titles at an eye-popping rate of 1.25 million copies a month.

Helen Thomas is the dean of the White House press corps. She has covered Watergate, Iran-Contra, and Whitewater, as well as every other aspect of the White House and the presidency since that of JFK. She is the author of *Dateline: White House* and *Front Row at the White House: My Life and Times.*

Bob Vila is the host of the highly successful television program, *Home Again*, which is syndicated to more than 175 stations nationwide by CBS Eyemark Entertainment. The show is currently in its ninth season.

Jack Welch, a native of Salem, Massachusetts, joined General Electric in 1960 and was elected vice-president in 1972, and vice-chairman in 1979. In 1981, he became the eighth chairman and CEO in GE's 118-year history.

George F. Will is an ABC News commentator, Pulitzer Prize winner, and author of a syndicated column that appears in more than 450 newspapers. He became a contributing editor of *Newsweek* magazine in 1976. One year later he was awarded the Pulitzer Prize for Commentary. He is the author of several books, most recently *Bunts: Curt Flood, Camden Yards, Pete Rose and Other Reflections on Baseball.*

Robin Williams, the brilliant comedian with amazing improvisational talents, has also proven himself to be a fine dramatic actor. His films include *Dead Poets Society* (1989), *Mrs. Doubtfire* (1993), and *Good Will Hunting,* (1997), in which he gave an Oscar-winning performance.

Kristi Yamaguchi was one of the first U.S. women to compete in both pairs' events and ladies' singles. She and her partner, Rudy Galindo, were the 1988 World Junior Pair Champions. In that same championship event, Kristi was also the Ladies' World Junior Champion. In 1992, she won her first U.S. National Championship. Kristi won a gold medal at the 1992 Olympics, the first U.S. woman to do so since Dorothy Hamill in 1976.